Hands-on Projects About
Earth and Space

Krista West

The Rosen Publishing Group's
PowerKids Press™
New York

Some of the projects in this book were designed for a child to do together with an adult.

Published in 2002 by The Rosen Publishing Group, Inc.
29 East 21st Street, New York, NY 10010

First Edition

Book Design: Michael de Guzman
Project Editors: Jennifer Landau, Jason Moring, Jennifer Quasha, Emily Raabe

Photo Credits: Cover (model and materials) © Cindy Reiman; p. 6 (materials) © Cindy Reiman; p. 7 (model and materials) © Cindy Reiman; p. 8 (materials) © Cindy Reiman; p. 9 (model and materials) © Cindy Reiman; p. 10 (materials) © Cindy Reiman; p. 11 (model and materials) © Cindy Reiman; p. 12 (materials) © Cindy Reiman; p. 13 (model and materials) © Cindy Reiman; p. 14 (materials) © Cindy Reiman; p. 15 (model and materials) © Cindy Reiman, (moon) Courtesy of NASA/JPL/California Institute of Technology ; p. 16 (materials) © Cindy Reiman, (moon) Courtesy of NASA/JPL/California Institute of Technology; p. 17 (model and materials) © Cindy Reiman, (moon) Courtesy of NASA/JPL/California Institute of Technology ; p. 18 (materials) © Cindy Reiman; p. 19 (model and materials) © Cindy Reiman, (background, the Milky Way) © Photri Inc.; p. 20 (materials) © Cindy Reiman; p. 21 (model and materials) © Cindy Reiman, (asteroid 1999JM8 depicted) © Reuters NewMedia Inc./CORBIS.

West, Krista.
Hands-on projects about earth and space / Krista West.
  p. cm. — (Great earth science projects)
ISBN 0-8239-5843-4
1. Astronomy—Experiments—Juvenile literature. [1. Astronomy—Experiments. 2. Earth—Experiments. 3. Experiments.] I. Title. II. Series.
QB46 .W435 2002
520—dc21
                                                                                                    00-012482

Manufactured in the United States of America

Contents

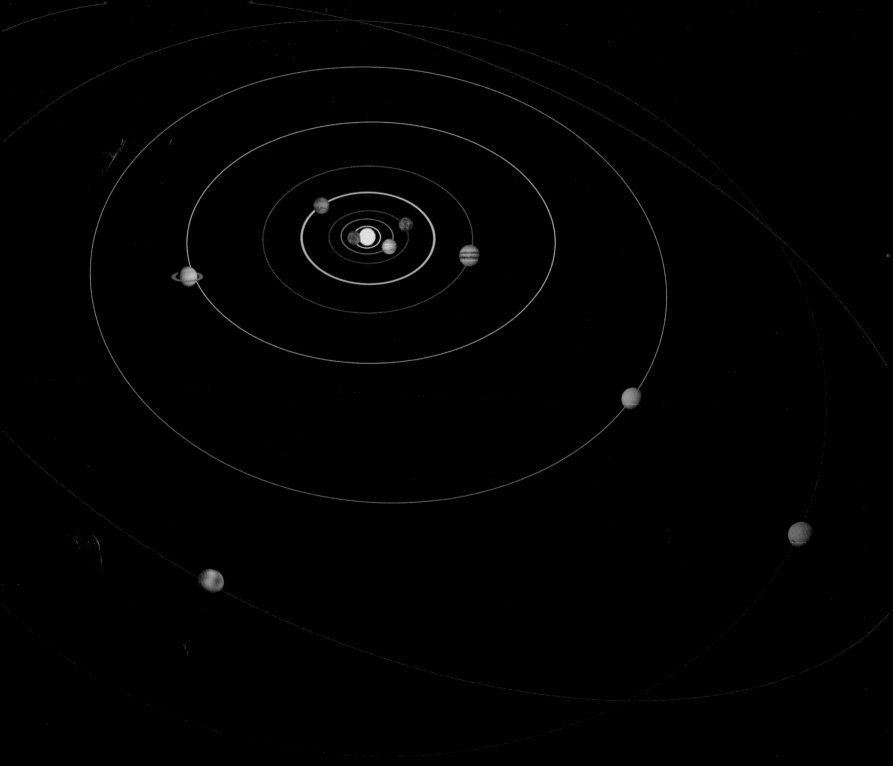

Get to Know Planet Earth

When you step on the ground, Earth appears to be solid, stationary, and flat. The Sun, Moon, and stars move across the sky and Earth seems to stand still. For a long time, these simple observations led people to think that Earth did not move and that it was the center of the universe. They were wrong.

Earth is only one of nine planets **orbiting** the Sun. The Sun is the center of our **solar system**. Earth is actually a spinning, round rock flying around the Sun at 66,000 miles per hour (106,217 km/h). That is almost four times the speed of the space shuttle, the vehicle astronauts use to fly in space.

On Earth we don't feel like we're moving because we move with Earth. However, we do feel the effects of **gravity**, or the force that attracts objects to one another.

— *Earth is one of nine planets orbiting the Sun.*

Make a Model of Our Solar System

Everything in our solar system, including planets, moons, stars, **asteroids**, and **comets**, orbits the Sun. The Sun is a star just like the ones we see at night, but it is much closer to Earth. We get our heat, light, and energy from the Sun. The nine planets that orbit the Sun are Mercury, Venus, Earth, Mars, Jupiter, Saturn, Uranus, Neptune, and Pluto. Earth is the third planet from the Sun, 93 million miles (150 million km) away. If you drive at 55 miles per hour (89 km/h) without stopping, it would take about 200 years to get there. Try making a model of our solar system and comparing the distances of different planets.

You will need
- A basketball
- A grapefruit
- An apple
- Two plums
- Two small marbles
- Two peas
- A kernel of unpopped popcorn

1 Find a long stretch of open space about 30 yards (27 m) long. Playgrounds and parks are good places. Walk to one end and put down the basketball. The basketball represents the Sun. Each object you use represents a planet. The size difference between the objects gives you an idea of the different size of the planets.

2 Starting at the basketball, take one step and put down a pea for Mercury. Take another step and put down a marble for Venus. Take a half step from Venus and put down the other marble for Earth, where we live. Each step you take represents about 36 million miles (58 million km).

3 From Earth, take one and a half steps and put down a pea for Mars. Now take nine steps and put down the grapefruit for Jupiter. Go eleven steps and set down the apple for Saturn.

4 Next comes Uranus. Walk twenty-four steps and put down a plum for Uranus. Take twenty-seven more steps and put down the other plum for Neptune. Finally, walk twenty-four steps and put down the popcorn kernel for Pluto, the ninth planet from the sun. Step back and take a look. You've mapped the planets in our solar system!

Draw an Orbit

As planets, moons, stars, asteroids, and comets orbit the Sun, they travel like spinning tops in oval shapes, called **ellipses**. It takes Earth 365 days, or one year, to complete one orbit around the Sun. Planets that are farther from the Sun have longer orbits. It takes Pluto 248 Earth years to travel around the Sun once. Most comets that orbit the Sun take thousands of years to complete one orbit, so we rarely get to see them. No matter how long the orbits are, they are always in the same oval shape. You can draw different orbits at home with a few simple supplies.

You will need	• Two thumbtacks • A piece of cardboard • 1 foot (30 cm) of string • Pencil and paper

Lay your piece of paper on the cardboard and stick 2 thumbtacks in the center, about 5 inches (13 cm) apart. One of the thumbtacks represents the Sun.

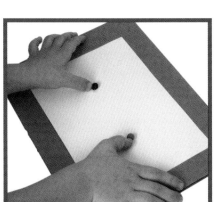

 Tie the ends of the string to make a circle. Loop it over the ends of the thumbtacks.

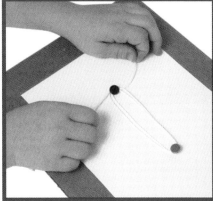

 Place your pencil in the loop of string with the point on the paper. Stretch it so it is tight.

 Slowly move your pencil around the thumbtacks, always keeping the pencil on the paper and the string tight. When you're done, you will have traced an ellipse, the shape that objects make when orbiting the Sun.

Measure Earth's Gravity

Gravity is the force that attracts one object to another. How strong the gravity is between two things depends on how heavy the objects are and how far apart they are. In our solar system, the Sun is so large and so close that its gravity keeps all the planets and stars in orbit. Earth's gravity keeps everything on our planet from flying into space, and it is what makes objects fall to the ground when we drop them. **Galileo Galilei**, a scientist who lived in the 1500s, found that all objects on Earth fall at the same rate because of gravity. You can see the effects of gravity by doing this simple experiment.

You will need
- A sturdy chair
- An orange
- A lemon
- Other droppable objects

Take the orange in one hand and the lemon in the other. Carefully step onto the seat of a sturdy chair.

 Extend both arms in front of you so that the orange and lemon are the same distance away from the ground.

Let them go at the same time. Which one hit the ground first? Gravity makes everything drop at the same rate, so the lemon and the orange should have hit the ground at the same time.

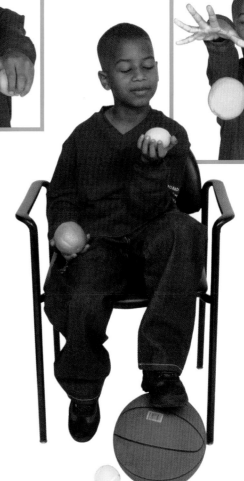

 Try it again with two balls. Then try it with a softball and a baseball. Some objects, such as feathers, won't work in this experiment because their shape slows their fall.

Explore Day and Night

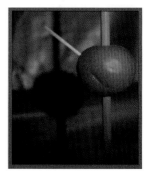

Everything in our solar system is constantly moving. Earth's movements explain why the Sun appears to move across the sky, why the Moon seems to change shape, and why we have days and nights. Earth spins in a complete circle once every 24 hours, the time length of one day. During this time, some parts of Earth face the Sun, making it daytime, while other parts face away from the Sun, making it night. Earth always spins in the same direction around its **axis**, an imaginary line through the North and South Poles. You can make a model of Earth and spin it on its axis to see why we have day and night.

You will need

- Clay
- A pencil
- A flashlight
- A toothpick
- A friend

1 Mold the clay into a round ball to represent Earth. Push the pencil through the middle of the ball so that it sticks out on both ends. The pencil represents Earth's axis. Stick one end of the toothpick into the ball of clay to mark where you live.

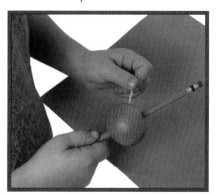

2 Have a friend stand in the middle of the room holding a flashlight. Turn the flashlight on and shine it straight ahead. The flashlight represents light from the Sun. Hold the ends of the pencil so that the clay Earth is in the flashlight beam.

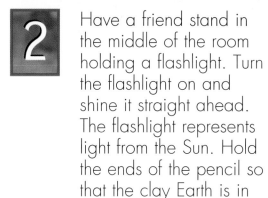

3 Where is the toothpick? One side of the clay Earth is lit by the "sun," making it daytime. The other side is dark, or nighttime.

4 Slowly spin the pencil in your hands and rotate the clay ball. Watch the shadows created by the toothpick as it rotates in and out of the flashlight beam. We see shadows similar to those on sunny days on Earth.

Discover Why the Moon Seems to Change Shape

You probably have noticed that the Moon seems to change shape in the sky. Sometimes it's a C-shaped sliver called a **crescent**. Sometimes it's a full, bright circle. Other times the Moon is nowhere to be found. We call these shape changes the **phases** of the Moon. These phases can be misleading because the Moon actually doesn't change shape or shine. As the Moon moves around Earth, different areas of the Moon are lit by the Sun so that we can see them. What we see depends on the position of the Moon to the Sun. You can recreate the phases of the Moon at home with some simple props. Try this experiment, then watch the Moon during the next month and see the phases change.

You will need

- A ball
- A cup
- A flashlight
- A dark room
- A friend

In a dark room, place a cup in the middle of a table and rest a ball on its rim. The ball represents the Moon.

 Pick a spot to sit about six steps from the ball. Then have a friend turn on a flashlight and shine it on the ball. The flashlight represents the Sun.

 Ask the friend to walk around the ball slowly, shining the flashlight on the ball. Look carefully at the ball to see which areas are lit as the "sun" moves. (Remember that in real life the Moon moves around the Sun.)

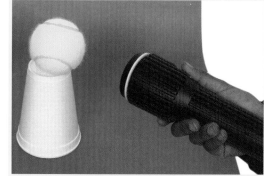

 Can you see the phases? Look for a crescent moon and a full moon.

Look at the Moon

    Earth's moon was formed when a large object struck Earth and broke off some bits of rock about 4.5 billion years ago. The rock circled Earth and then came together to form the Moon. As the Moon formed, it was hit by **meteoroids**, or rocks flying through space. These meteoroids became **meteorites** when they crashed into the Moon's surface. The meteorites created **craters** all over the Moon. You can see the edges of the craters along the **terminator**. Take a look at the Moon and see if you can find any of these features.

You will need

- Binoculars
- A bath towel
- A clear night when the Moon is about half full
- A clear night when the Moon is nearly half full
- A parent or friend

1 Go outside on a clear night when the Moon is nearly full. Lie down on your towel and, using the binoculars, look at the Moon.

2 When the Moon is nearly full, look for long streaks of light-colored rocks. These rays are splatter marks made when meteoroids crashed into the Moon. Next look for dark patches on the Moon. This is hardened lava.

3 Go outside on another night when the Moon is half full. Again lie down on your towel, using your binoculars to look at the Moon.

4 This time look at the terminator, the line between the dark and light parts of the Moon. Look carefully for bumps and ridges along the line. These are the edges of craters.

Make Your Own Star Map

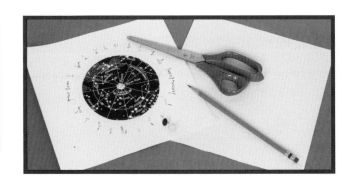

Star maps are used to locate stars and known patterns of stars, called **constellations**, in the sky at different times of the year. Which stars you see will depend on where you live and when you look. As Earth moves around the Sun, different groups of stars move in and out of view. In the Northern Hemisphere, we see a small group of stars all year long. This is because Earth's axis points directly at the North Star, called Polaris. You can make a star map to locate the stars at different times of the year.

You will need
- Photocopy of star map
- Pencil and paper
- Scissors
- A brass tack
- An adult

Go to the reference section of your local library and ask your librarian for a star map of the Northern Hemisphere. Photocopy the map. Remember to copy down the months of the year in their correct positions on the map.

 Cut your copied star chart into a circle. From another piece of paper, cut out a slightly larger circle and write the times of the day as shown. Don't forget to write TOP near 12:00 P.M. and BOTTOM near 12:00 A.M.

 Place the star chart circle on top of the circle with the times of day and attach them at the center with a bent paper clip. You should be able to move the circles around. This is a star map that you can use to locate stars in the sky.

 Pick a clear night when the stars are visible and go outside. On your star map, spin the circles so that the time of night when you are outside lines up with the month of the year. Hold your star map with the TOP pointed toward the sky. Have an adult help you face north and look for the patterns of stars on your map. Can you find them?

Experiment with Asteroid Shapes

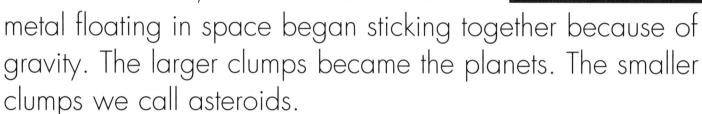

When our solar system was formed, scientists believe, chunks of rock and metal floating in space began sticking together because of gravity. The larger clumps became the planets. The smaller clumps we call asteroids.

An asteroid that leaves its orbit and travels through space is called a meteoroid. Some meteoroids reach the surface of Earth to become meteorites. You can experiment with shapes of asteroids and bake them to make "meteorites." Ask an adult for help with this project.

You will need

- Milk or butter (optional)
- A large pot ¾ full of water
- Stove top
- Mixer or potato masher
- Greased cookie sheet
- Oven
- Six large peeled potatoes
- An adult to help

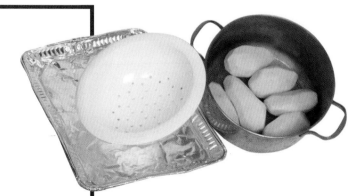

Boil the peeled potatoes in a pot on the stove until they are soft. Drain the water.

 Mix or mash the potatoes until you have a sticky, white substance. You may need to add some milk or butter if the potatoes are too hard.

 Mold the potatoes with your hands to create the shapes of asteroids. Can you make some of the shapes on this page?

 Place your asteroid shapes made from potatoes on a greased cookie sheet and bake them at 375 degrees for 20 minutes. They will become a darker color, much like asteroids that hit Earth and become meteorites.

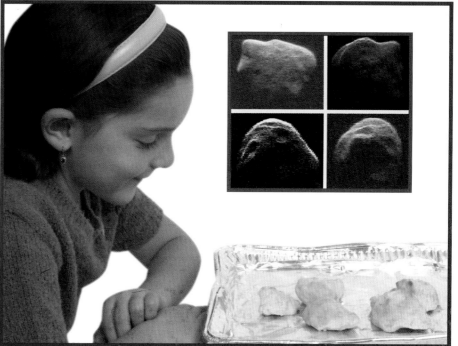

Other Solar Systems

As you start to think more and more about Earth and its place in our solar system, it starts to feel like a huge, unexplored place. Are there more planets circling our sun that we haven't yet discovered? Will humankind ever set foot on Mars? Does life exist on other planets? The questions are nearly endless, and scientists around the world are constantly working to understand more about our solar system and those beyond. They use math, technology, and imagination to do their jobs. If you think you might like to be a space scientist someday, you're off to a good start.

Glossary

asteroids (AS-teh-roydz) Small bodies made of rocks and iron that revolve around the sun.

axis (AK-sis) A straight line on which an object turns or seems to turn.

comets (KAH-mits) Bodies made of ice and dust that look like stars with tails of light.

constellations (kon-stuh-LAY-shunz) Officially recognized patterns of stars in the night sky.

craters (KRAY-terz) Holes in the ground, shaped like bowls.

crescent (KREH-sent) C-shaped portion of a circle.

ellipses (ih-LIP-seez) Oval shapes.

Galileo Galilei (gah-lih-LAY-oh gah-li-LAY) An Italian physicist and astronomer who invented the telescope and experimented with motion.

gravity (GRA-vih-tee) The natural force that attracts one object to another.

meteorites (MEE-tee-uh-rytes) Rocks that have reached Earth from outer space.

meteoroids (MEE-tee-uh-roydz) Clumps of rock that are travelling through space.

orbiting (OR-bih-ting) When one thing is circling another.

phases (FAY-zez) Apparent changes in an object, in this case, the shape of the moon.

solar system (SOH-ler SIS-tem) A group of planets that circles a star.

star maps (STAR MAPS) Maps used to locate stars in the sky.

terminator (TER-mih-nay-ter) The line that divides the light and dark sides of the moon.

Index

Web Sites

To learn more about earth and space, check out these Web sites:
www.astronomy.com
www.skypub.com
www.theskyguide.com